EXPERIMENTS WITH ENERGY

By Anna Claybourne

WINDMILL BOOKS

OCT 2016

DISCARD

W9-BUI-491

Published in 2017 by **Windmill Books,** an Imprint of Rosen Publishing
29 East 21st Street, New York, NY 10010

Copyright © Arcturus Holdings Limited

All rights reserved. No part of this book may be reproduced in any form
without permission in writing from the publisher, except by a reviewer.

Author: Anna Claybourne
Designer: Emma Randall
Illustrations: Caroline Romanet

CATALOGING-IN-PUBLICATION DATA

Names: Claybourne, Anna.
Title: Experiments with energy / Anna Claybourne.
Description: New York : Windmill Books, 2017. | Series: First science experiments |
    Includes index.
Identifiers: ISBN 9781508192411 (pbk.) | ISBN 9781508192374 (library bound) |
    ISBN 9781508192299 (6 pack)
Subjects: LCSH: Force and energy--Experiments--Juvenile literature.
Classification: LCC QC73.4 C627 2017 | DDC 530--dc23

Manufactured in the United States of America
CPSIA Compliance Information: Batch #BS16PK: For Further Information contact Rosen Publishing, New York, New York at 1-800-237-9932

R0447115256

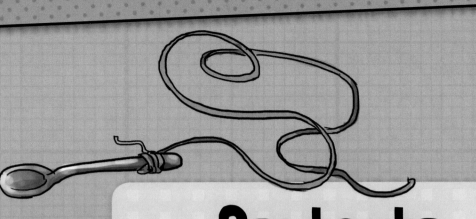

Contents

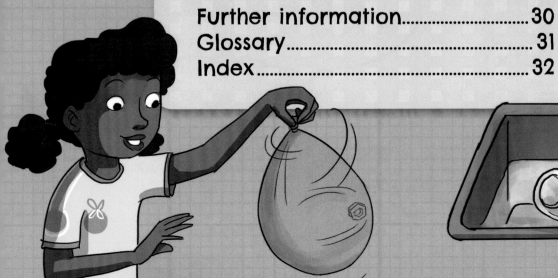

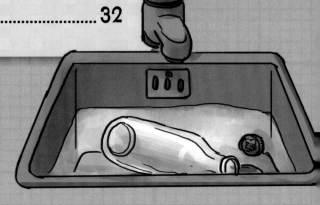

Introduction

Science means finding out about the world, and all the stuff in it. That's why scientists do experiments – to find out as much as they can!

Science tips

- Clear a neat, empty space for doing experiments in.
- Check if it's OK to use the things in the "You will need" boxes with whoever owns them!
- For messy experiments, wear old clothes, not your best outfit!
- Do messy experiments outdoors, if you can.
- Remember to clean up the mess afterwards!

GET AN ADULT ASSISTANT

For some of the experiments, you'll need to heat things, cook things, chop things up, or use electrical items. For anything like this, make sure you have an adult handy to help you..

KEEPING RECORDS

Real scientists don't just do experiments - they also keep records. To do this, you could take photos of your experiments or draw pictures of them, and write down what happened.

Try it yourself!

This book is full of easy but exciting experiments for you to try for yourself. For most of them, you only need a few basic things that you can find at home.

Are you ready to experiment? Turn the page and let's get started!

Energy

Energy is what makes things happen. When things move, heat up, make a noise, or glow with light, it takes energy to make them work. Energy is everywhere – without it, nothing would happen at all!

You take in energy when you eat food, and use it to make your body move.

Round and round

Energy does not get "used up." It just changes from one form into another. For example, a candle contains chemical energy. When it burns, the chemical energy turns into heat and light energy.

There are many types, or "forms", of energy. Most of them are things you experience every day. Here are some of the main forms of energy:

Heat - the hotter something is, the more energy is in it.

Light - a form of energy that we can sense with our eyes

Sound - a form of energy that we can sense with our ears

Movement - all movement is a form of energy.

Chemical energy - the energy stored in food and fuel

Electricity - we use this to power machines.

Try this!
Try these everyday activities to see energy at work.

Switch on a flashlight. It uses electrical energy from the battery to make light glow.

Rub your hands together fast. You put in movement energy, and your hands warm up.

Hit a pan with a wooden spoon. You put in movement energy, using your arm. It turns into sound energy.

Heat is movement

When things are hot, it actually means they are moving more. These experiments will show you how!

You will need:

· Hot tap water (not too hot to touch)
· Cold water
· Two glasses
· Three bowls
· Food coloring
· Two hands

1 Half-fill one glass with hot tap water, and the other with cold water. Stand them side by side.

Another fun idea
Instead of food coloring, try mixing in sugar. Does it dissolve faster in hot water, or cold?

2 Drop one drop of food coloring into each glass. Watch them closely. What happens?

3 Now half-fill one bowl with hot water, and another with cold water. Stand them side by side.

4 In the third bowl, mix equal amounts of hot and cold water to make lukewarm water.

5 Put one hand in the hot water and the other in the cold water, and leave them there for one minute.

6 Now take both your hands out and put them together into the bowl of lukewarm water. How does it feel?

What has happened?

The food coloring spreads out faster in the hot water than in the cold water. That's because when the water is warmer, its molecules (the tiny parts it is made of) contain more movement energy. They move faster, and push the food coloring around.

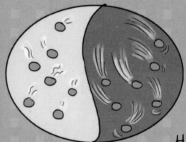

Colder

Hotter

Hot and cold hands

When warmer and colder things meet, the movement in the warmer things pushes against the colder things, and warms them up. Your hands aren't very good at sensing temperature. Instead, they sense whether they are losing heat energy, or getting more. The cold hand is getting more heat energy, so it feels warm. The warm hand is losing heat energy, so it feels cold.

Getting bigger

When things get hotter, the molecules in them move faster. That makes them push away from each other, and they take up more space.

You will need:

· A bag of marshmallows
· A microwaveable plate
· A microwave oven
· A glass bottle
· A coin that covers the opening of the bottle
· A sink with hot and cold taps

THE MIGHTY MARSHMALLOW

1 First, microwave your marshmallow. Put one marshmallow on the plate, and put it in the microwave.

2 Switch the microwave on, on normal power, for 10-15 seconds. Open the door as soon as it stops.

3 Compare the marshmallow with another one from the bag. What's the difference?

Watch out!
The marshmallow could be very hot at first. You can eat it, but wait for it to cool for a minute before you do!

10

BOTTLE BLAST

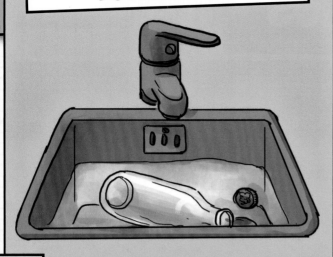

1   Run cold water into the sink. Put the glass bottle and the coin in to get nice and cold.

2   Empty the bottle and stand it up. Put the wet coin over the top of it.

3   Run hot water into the sink to make a shallow bath, and stand the bottle in it. What happens?

Another fun idea
What happens if you put a balloon over the neck of the bottle?

What has happened?

Marshmallows contain lots of tiny air bubbles. As they heat up, the molecules in the air move faster, and push against each other. The air bubbles get bigger, making the marshmallow grow. The same thing happens inside the bottle. The air warms up and gets bigger. It pushes at the coin on top of the bottle, making it jump.

Magic marbles

The energy of a moving marble can behave in a strange way!

1 Fold the card stock in half down the middle, then make two more folds the other way to make a channel, like this.

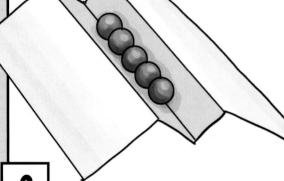

2 Put your marbles in a row in the channel, like this. They should all be touching each other.

3 Roll one marble back away from the others, then flick it gently towards them. What do you think will happen?

What has happened?

When the moving marble hits the others, they don't all move! Only the one on the other end does. As the first marble hits the second, it passes movement energy into it. The second hits the third, the third hits the fourth, and so on, all passing their energy on. Only the last marble moves, because it has space to.

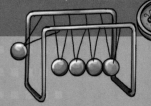

This toy, called Newton's cradle, works the same way.

Sound is movement

How can you make a balloon buzz?
Try this experiment.

1 Put the nut inside the balloon. Blow up the balloon until it's quite big, then tie it closed.

You will need:

· A balloon
· A hexagonal lug nut, like this.

Watch out!
Keep the nut in the bottom of the balloon, away from your mouth, as you blow.

2 Hold the balloon by the top and move it around in a circle, to make the nut whirl around inside. Can you hear a buzz?

Another fun idea
Put your hands around the balloon, and hold it up to a working radio speaker. You'll feel it vibrating!

What has happened?

Sound is a form of energy that is made when objects vibrate, or move quickly to and fro. As the nut whirls around, its corners bump against the balloon, making it vibrate very quickly. This makes a high buzzing sound!

Sound in a spoon!

In this experiment, you can find out how the same noise can sound very different, depending on how it travels.

You will need:

· String
· Scissors
· Two metal spoons

1 Cut a piece of string about as long as your arm. Tie one end around the handle of one of the spoons.

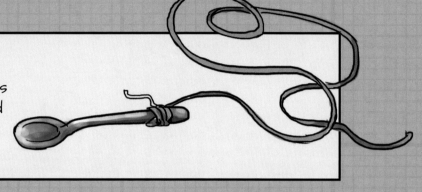

2 Hold the other end of the string so that the spoon is dangling, then hit the spoon with the other spoon.

3 What kind of noise does it make? Is it easy to hear? What does it remind you of?

4

Now wrap the end of the string around the tip of your finger, and press your finger against your ear.

Watch out!
You don't need to stick your finger right inside your ear, as this can be bad for your ear. Just press it against your ear.

5

Hit the spoon again. Does it sound different? What is different about it?

Another fun idea
Try tying two or more spoons to a longer piece of string. Hold both ends to your ears – or have two people listen to one end each!

What has happened?

Our ears hear sounds because the vibrations that make the sound spread out through the air. The spoon vibrates, it makes the air vibrate, and the vibrations (called sound waves) hit your ears.

But when you press the string against your ear, the sound vibrations spread to your ear along the string, and through your finger and your head. Sound waves travel much faster and better through solid things than they do through air. So this way, the spoon noise sounds louder and stronger.

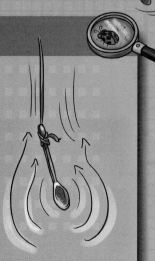

See a sound before you hear it

Sound takes time to travel through the air. Light moves much more quickly than sound, and that means you can sometimes see someone making a noise before you hear anything!

1 First, measure out a big distance on the ground. If it's too hard to measure, you could just take big steps and count the number of steps.

29...30!

You will need:

- A friend or family member to help
- Two old pans or other noisy metal objects, such as buckets
- A very big open space
- A stopwatch or smartphone timer
- A tape measure (optional)

2 One person stands at one end with the two pans. The other stands at the other end with the stopwatch, ready to start it. You must be able to see each other!

3 The person with the pans should hold them wide apart, then bash them together. At the moment they touch, the other person should start the stopwatch.

Try this!
Can you use math to work out how fast the sound was moving?

What has happened?

When something makes a sound, the sound vibrations spread out through the air. This means you don't hear sounds right away – it takes a little while for them to travel to you. When you are close to things, it happens quickly and you don't notice it. But when you are far away, you can see something noisy happening, but not hear it until a little while later.

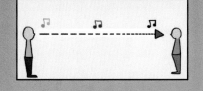

4 The person with the stopwatch should stop it as soon as they hear the crash of the pans being banged together. How long did the sound take to reach them?

Make a rainbow

Light usually looks white or yellowish, but it is actually made up of all the colors of the rainbow. Here's how to see them.

1 Place the container in bright direct sunlight (either outdoors, or by a window where the Sun is shining in).

You will need:

· A bright, sunny day
· A small mirror (that you can get wet)
· A piece of white paper or card stock
· A shallow plastic container
· Water

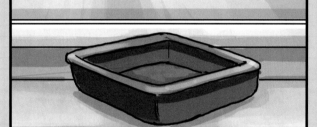

2 Pour water into the container until it is as deep as the size of the mirror. Put the mirror into the water.

3 Position the mirror so that the Sun shines onto it. Position the white card stock to catch the light reflected from the mirror.

Watch out!

Remember not to look directly at the Sun, or at the reflected sunlight – it can damage your eyes.

4 Gently tilt and move the mirror to get the best position. You should see a pattern of rainbow colors on the card stock.

Another fun idea

You can also make a rainbow using a garden hose on a sunny day. Stand with your back to the Sun, and spray a fine mist of water. You should see a rainbow appear in the mist.

What has happened?

White light, like the light that shines from the Sun, is made up of a range, or spectrum, of different colors. When light passes in and out of different see-through substances, such as water and air, it bends, or refracts. The different colors of light bend different amounts. This makes them separate out from each other, and appear as a rainbow of colors.

Scientists use a shaped piece of glass called a prism to split light into its colors.

Make a periscope

Light reflects, or bounces, off mirrors. You can use this to help you look around a corner, by making a periscope!

You will need:

- A long cardboard box or container, such as a plastic wrap or plastic bag box
- Two small mirrors that will fit inside the box
- Modeling clay or sticky tack
- Marker
- Scissors

1 Open the side of the box so that you can see what you are doing. Some boxes will have a lid that opens, like this.

2 Mark two windows on the box - one at one end, and one at the other end on the opposite side. Carefully cut them out.

3 Put a large blob of clay or sticky tack inside the corner opposite each window. Press the blobs into the corners.

4 Press the two mirrors onto the blobs so that they are positioned diagonally opposite the windows.

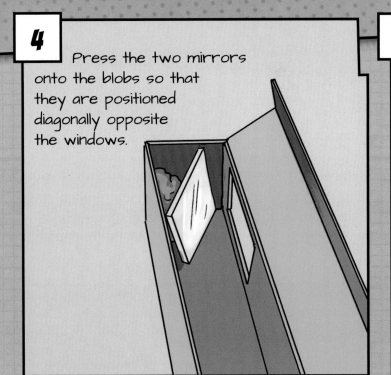

5 You should now be able to look into one window, and see out of the other. If you can't, adjust the angles of the mirrors until it works.

6 Close the side of the box. Your periscope is ready! You can use it to look around a corner or over a wall.

What has happened?

Light travels in straight lines. When it hits a mirror, it bounces off. If the mirror is flat, the light will bounce back the way it came. But if the mirror is at an angle, the light will bounce off in a different direction. The angled mirrors make light coming in at one window bounce along the tube, and travel out of the other window.

The broken straw

How can a straw be whole, but look as if it's in two pieces? All you need is water.

You will need:

- A glass
- A straw
- Water

1 Fill the glass with water almost to the top.

2 Put the straw into the water so that it leans over sideways.

Did you know?
Objects like straws don't shine with light. But you see them because light from the Sun, or a lamp, bounces off them and enters your eyes.

3 Look at the straw from the side. What has happened to it?

What has happened?

The straw is just the same as it always was, but it looks different. This is because of refraction – the way light bends when it passes in or out of something see-through. Part of the straw is in the air, and the light from it comes straight to your eyes. Part of it is in the water, and the light from it bends as it moves through water and glass on its way to you. So the two parts look as if they are in different places.

The shrinking legs

Refraction can also make things look bigger or smaller than they are. Make a swimming pool for a toy, and see its legs shrink!

You will need:

- A few plastic toy figures (that can get wet)
- A shallow container or dish
- Water

1 Pour water into the tray or dish until it is about waist-deep for your toy figures.

2 Stand the toys in their "swimming pool." Now look at them from just above and to one side.

Try this!
You may be able to see this happening to real people's legs too, when they are in a swimming pool or paddling pool.

3 What has happened to their legs? Take them in and out of the water to see the difference.

What has happened?

As light from the toys' legs moves out of the water into the air, it bends. When you see it, it looks as if it has come from higher up, making the toys legs look shorter.

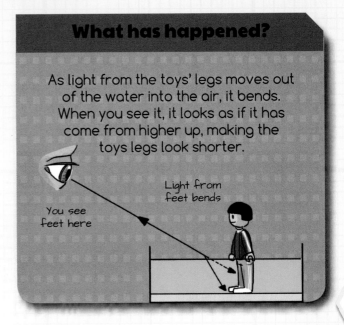

You see feet here

Light from feet bends

Sparks in the dark

Light shines from the Sun and stars, lamps, candles and TV screens. But there's another, very strange kind of light that can come from things being crushed or ripped.

You will need:

- Sugar cubes
- A clear sandwich bag
- Pliers
- Duct tape, packing tape or adhesive tape
- Self-seal envelopes
- A very dark area

1 First, set up a dark area. It could be a room with a blackout blind, a dark garden at night, or you could make a dark den under a large blanket.

2 Prepare your experiments with the light on, before taking them into the dark to try out. Wait in the dark for a few minutes before you start, to help your eyes see the sparks better.

TEST 1:

Preparation: Put some sugar cubes in the sandwich bag. Seal it closed. Stick two strips of tape together, with the ends apart and folded over. Seal the envelope closed.

Using the pliers, crush the sugar cubes through the bag, and look for flashes of light as they break apart. (Don't nip your fingers! You might want to get an adult to do this job.)

TEST 2:

Take your sealed self-seal envelope, and pull open the seal. You may see sparks of light where the glue comes apart.

TEST 3:

Hold the two folded ends of the tape, and rip them apart. Can you see light glowing? Sometimes, pulling tape from the roll can also make light.

What has happened?

This kind of light has a long name – triboluminescence (say try-boe-loo-min-ess-ens). It happens when some types of chemicals break apart.

Static electric games

Electricity is a form of energy. One type of electricity is called static. It can build up in objects and make them behave in weird ways.

TO BEGIN...

Rub the balloon several times on the woolly surface. Only rub in one direction, then lift the balloon and rub again.

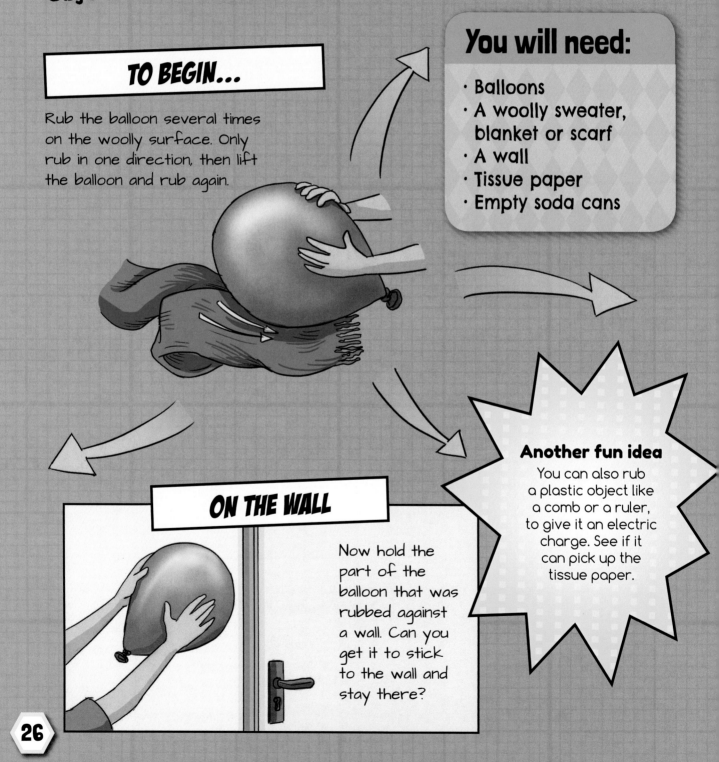

You will need:

- Balloons
- A woolly sweater, blanket or scarf
- A wall
- Tissue paper
- Empty soda cans

Another fun idea

You can also rub a plastic object like a comb or a ruler, to give it an electric charge. See if it can pick up the tissue paper.

ON THE WALL

Now hold the part of the balloon that was rubbed against a wall. Can you get it to stick to the wall and stay there?

HAIR-RAISING

Rub the balloon on your hair. Then slowly lift the balloon up... and it should pull your hair up with it!

PICK UP BITS

Tear some tissue paper into tiny pieces. Rub the balloon on the wool again, then hold it over the tissue paper. Does it pull them up like a magnet?

CAN RACE

For this experiment, you need two people. Lay two empty soda cans on their sides. Rub two balloons on the woolly surface. Hold the balloons near the cans, and they will start to roll. Who can make theirs go fastest?

What has happened?

Objects contain tiny parts called electrons, which can move. Moving electrons make electricity. When you rub the balloon on the wool, some electrons move from the wool into the balloon. This makes an electrical pull, or charge, between the balloon and other objects.

Thinking about... energy

A thermometer like this works because things get bigger as they heat up. When it gets warmer, the liquid in the tube gets bigger. It takes up more space, and pushes along the tube.

Sound is made when things vibrate. If you play a musical instrument, think about what is vibrating to make the sound. It could be strings, your lips, a reed in a mouthpiece, or a drumskin.

A real rainbow in the sky happens when sunlight shines into falling raindrops. The light refracts, or bends, as it moves in and out of each water droplet. This splits the light into a spectrum of colors.

You might see solar panels like these on roofs. They collect light energy from the Sun, and turn it into a supply of electricity that people can use inside their houses.

Further information

Books

Disgusting and Dreadful Science: Electric Shocks and Other Energy Evils by Anna Claybourne (Franklin Watts, 2014)

Earth Cycles: Energy by Jillian Powell (Franklin Watts, 2014)

Eyewitness: Energy by Jack Challoner (DK Children, 2016)

The Science of Roller Coasters: Understanding Energy by Karen Latchana Kenney (Checkerboard, 2016)

Websites

For web resources related to the subject of this book, go to: www.windmillbooks.com/weblinks and select this book's title.

Glossary

chemical energy
Energy released by chemicals reacting to each other.

electrons
Tiny particles of matter with a negative electrical charge.

hexagonal
The description of a shape that has six angles and six sides.

magnet
An object that is able to pull some types of metal towards it.

molecules
The smallest part of a substance that is still defined as that substance. For example, a water molecule is the smallest unit of water that is still water.

periscope
A long tube with mirrors inside that is used to look over or around objects.

prism
A triangular chunk of glass or clear plastic that separates light that passes through it into different colors.

refraction
The bending of a ray of light as it passes through one substance into another, such as from air into water.

sound wave
A vibration that is produced when a sound is made, and is responsible for carrying sounds to the ear.

spectrum
The group of different colors that are separated out from a ray of light.

static
A form of electricity that is produced by friction.

thermometer
An instrument used for measuring temperature.

triboluminescence
The light produced by friction that causes some chemicals to break apart.

vibrate
To move from side to side, or back and forth, very quickly.

vibrations
Continuous shaking movements.

Index